PRIESTHOOD

—◆—— VERSUS ——◆—

PARENTHOOD

Guidance and wisdom for those who bear the responsibility of serving God

CAPTAIN MOTHER
OLUFUNMILAYO HASSON

Mereo Books

1A The Wool Market Dyer Street Cirencester Gloucestershire GL7 2PR
An imprint of Memoirs Book Ltd. www.mereobooks.com

Priesthood versus Parenthood: 978-1-86151-928-3

First published in Great Britain in 2019
by Mereo Books, an imprint of Memoirs Books Ltd.

The address for Memoirs Books Ltd. can be
found at www.memoirspublishing.com

Memoirs Books Ltd. Reg. No. 7834348

Typeset in 11/15pt Century Schoolbook
by Wiltshire Associates Ltd.
Printed and bound in Great Britain by Biddles Books

PREFACE

The title of this book speaks for itself, but the contents speak for all its readers who are ordained servants of God and caring mentors to their fellow humans. They will open your eyes to the collaborative efforts between divinity and humanity.

Both priesthood and parenthood have their burdens, their challenges and their dangers. However, we need to appraise ourselves by asking some personal questions. Firstly, Why am I in the service of God? Did God call me into His vineyard as a Minister? Am I serving for self-security – what's in it for me? Do I have a private and personal agenda?

In this book, Captain Mother Olufunmilayo Hasson addresses these questions and provides answers and a way forward.

CONTENTS

ACKNOWLEDGEMENTS

My sincere appreciation to God, my Creator, for filling me with wit and wisdom to encourage and enlighten me not to bury what I need to expose.

My thanks to all around me, my loving husband, Hugh, children and friends, who have contributed immensely in assisting me to expose my talents.

This book is dedicated to those servants of God who, having spent their entire lives working in His vineyard by rendering services to mankind, have still paid the highest price of condemnation, victimization and rejection by man. It is dedicated to priests, prophets of old, present-day pastors and spiritualists who have used their instincts and the creativities inside them endlessly to the end, in their services to oneness in Church, Faith and God.

CHAPTER ONE

HEIRS OF PRIESTHOOD

The title of this book speaks for itself, but the contents will speak for all readers who are ordained servants of God and caring mentors to their fellow humans. The contents of this book will open your eyes to the collaborative efforts between divinity and humanity.

Both priesthood and parenthood have their burdens, their challenges, their dangers and their 'awkward smiles'. However, we need to appraise ourselves by asking some personal questions. Firstly ask yourself, Why am I in the service of God? Did God call me into His vineyard as a minister? Am I serving for self-security – what's in it for me? Do I have a private and personal agenda?

Whether we like it or not, there will always come a time when God will ask us the same question as He did Prophet Elijah **(1st Kings 19, verse 13: "And behold, there came a voice unto him, and said, What does thou here, Elijah?")**

What are we hungry for? Are we following and serving God because what we hunger for is in His hands? Is our desire of the flesh and the mind? In the Old Testament, God fed the Israelites with manna in the wilderness. In the New Testament, Jesus Christ fed thousands with the five loaves and two fishes. For our part, we must make our own contributions by humbling our pride and putting some sweat into the service which we render in His vineyard. When He is pleased with us, then He will recognise our hard work and give us a ministry and not a mystery; our ministerial efforts will succeed with strategic success rather than struggle.

Modern-day pastors pray constantly and ceaselessly, even encouraging our little children to speak in 'tongues'. Young and innocent children are being intentionally groomed to replace laziness with prayers. We have in our hands the case of a good son but bad parentage. Prayers will never replace laziness. It is arrant nonsense, leading young and upcoming Christians into believing that there is no human responsibility required in spiritual and miracle growth. This is impossible. It is not the money that you leave a child that makes him wealthy; it is what you leave in him or her.

Now is the time for all Christian leaders to put things right; we have the responsibility to correct the wrong notions. As leaders, there is nothing holding us up except our selfish and gullible pride, in making amends by preaching and teaching the truth that our miracles require hard work from us.

Our life is the direct result of what we do even as we operate in the spiritual realm. We believe that we receive in spirit and it happens naturally.

Both old and young, we all have our dreams. It is only with hard work and faith that our dreams will lead us to our goals in life. However, dreams without hard work lead to frustration. Our Creator does not mind us acquiring wealth; He minds wealth acquiring us. Therefore, we need more to serve; we need His Holy Spirit to keep us in line and in check. The Holy Spirit lives in us and He searches our minds and knows our intentions. The Holy Spirit makes us effective. He gives us power. We must rely on Him for guidance.

Most of us present-day Christians have been raised with the spirit of acquiring gifts and fruits from God. We are all smelling of guilt. If you want to know what's wrong with you, just look at your friends. We are surrounded by our situations.

We are not in a relationship with God; we are only interested in money, cars, houses, partners, and other worldly comfortable things that our positions in Christ can give us. Foolishly we quote the **Book of John 15 (verse 16): "You have not chosen me, but I have chosen you, that you should go and bring forth fruit and that your fruit should remain; that whatsoever you shall ask of the Father in my name, He may give it to you"**.

For the above to be applicable to us, we must comply with previous verses of the same Book and Chapter. The first verse reads **"I am the true vine, and my Father is the vine dresser"** says the Lord Jesus Christ. Here, Christ introduces us to the existing relationship between Himself, Christ the Son and God the Father. Here parenthood and priesthood are clarified. Our love for God, the Father and our passion for Christ His Son must be our driving force to take us into their comfortable hands.

The life of Moses, the Servant of God, in the Old Testament was an example for all believers. Extracts from the Holy Book Exodus 18 (verses 2–5) **"Then Jethro, Moses' father in law, took Zipporah, Moses' wife after he had sent her back. And her two sons; ...And Jethro, Moses' father in law, came with his sons and his wife unto Moses into the wilderness, where he encamped at the mount of God"**. This is an undisputed confirmation that Moses was a husband, a father and a family man. He fulfilled all parental responsibilities to his children. At no time did he use his office as a servant of God to accumulate wealth for his children. He did not groom his sons for priesthood roles. Contrary to general practice amongst the pastors, prophets and spiritual leaders of today, there was no promissory gain attached to his duties to his people, the Israelites and his God, Jehovah.

God did not lay it down for Moses' sons to inherit their father's spiritual cum leadership position. Rather, Joshua his servant was chosen by God to replace him. In the Book of **Numbers Chapter 21 (verses 22 – 23): "And Moses did as the Lord commanded him: and he took Joshua, and set him before Eleazar the priest, and before all the congregation. And gave him a charge, as the Lord commanded by the hand of Moses".**

Therefore, Joshua the son of Nun was filled with the Spirit of wisdom from God because Moses, the servant of God, had laid his hands on him. The transfer of the leadership role was ordered by God. The Almighty God instructed Moses to lay his mantle on Joshua his servant, thereby passing all powers and authorities of leadership to him. When we bless someone when there is nothing in it for us, then God will bless us abundantly.

However, at present in the Christian world, the opposite is the practice. Pastoral leadership is now regarded as a birthright and therefore it is seen as an inheritance by the children of the leaders with the **"Keep it in the Family"** slogan. We crave for assets. This is religion at the expense of social reality; it is brutal. We, the elder pastors, must accept our destiny and not allow our fate to change the destiny of oncoming younger pastors. Anything we do in the daytime that keeps us awake in the night will definitely hunt us, even in our graves. It is not easy to change our ways, but sometimes it is required. Let us surrender to fate and grace. It is not too late – we should do it now.

Let us all learn from the example set for us by God through Moses, and accept that leadership succession or the transfer of leadership powers should not be regarded as investing in our dreams. Racing the next generation in line of God, we must ensure we are not breeding a race of young megamillionaire pastors in a welfare situation. As anointed Servants of God, our roles must be seen to be helping our wards and congregations to find their destiny and not appointing or grooming them to fulfil ours.

After training, they have seen their destiny. It is now time to let go of them, leave them to go after their destiny. It is not always true that a child continues the legacy of his father. Our contributions to their lives must be constructive, not destructive. Release your children and wards with prayers for God to make a transfer of abundant blessings and victories into their lives so that they become greater and better than you in their chosen fields.

CHAPTER TWO

TEACHING WITH FEAR AND FAITH

There must be a clean and clear spirit of transparency between priests and their wards such that existed between Eli, the prophet of God and Samuel, his ward. Rearing with parental values and guiding with divine interventions will eventually lead to our efforts being recognised and set us free from our own human deprivation. As Elders in the Church holding the posts of authority, we must sacrifice our own habits for our callings to succeed.

Samuel was a child when he was called. He was not aware of his surroundings, but Eli, being the elder prophet, was there to guide him. Strict as he was, he was frank with Samuel to the core.

At his first assignment, Samuel was hesitant to deliver his spiritual message and revelation to his Master, but when he rebuked him in the name of the Almighty God, Samuel succumbed. The **Book of 1st Samuel Chapter 3 (verses 17-18): "And he said, What is the thing that the Lord has said unto thee? I pray thee hide it not from me. God do so to thee, and more also, if thou hide anything from me of all the things that God said unto thee".** At this point, both Eli and Samuel were almost divided by what they believed in.

As Elders in the house of God, we are more valuable at our age than the growing generation at their own early stage. We must exercise the spirit of discipline in teaching and training and desist from excuses to comfort our incapacity. We cannot afford to be frightening leaders.

Our experience in the service of God puts us a step ahead of our wards. We must teach and show the growing generation reference to God, with fear and faith. We are attracted to what we are exposed to. Children need to know that their commitment to God's work starts with their obedience to you as their earthly leaders. They must serve to be served. Their services to God start with respectable caring for fellow man and obedience to constituted authorities. Our ministerial position should not be seen as a quest for power or wealth acquisition.

We are all walking towards our future goals and definitely we shall live in what we build. Are we building a mess and asking God to condone it? He will not.

The competency of leadership must be fixed and corrected before it affects and destroys our destiny.

In bringing up our children and our wards, who are the next generation, we are building and carrying our future along with us. Whoever you run with is who you are. So when in the future you see your child as a minister in charge of your local church, the silent spirit within you will be saying "Here comes your monster and here lives your disaster," or "Here comes your pride and joy". The decision is yours. The **Book of Proverbs, Chapter 22 (verse 6), says "Train a child in the way he should go, and when he is old, he will not depart from it".**

The relationship between and Elijah and Elisha is worthy of emulation. Elisha served his master Elijah obediently without turning back. The **Holy Book, 2nd Kings, Chapter 3 (verse 11): "But Jehoshaphat said, is there not here a prophet of the Lord, that we may enquire of the Lord by him? And one of the King of Israel's servants answered and said, Here is Elisha the son of Shaphat, who poured water on the hands of Elijah".** To any God-fearing mind, this is the greatest description of total surrender and submission to high authority.

There is abundant reward in stewardship. Mentoring requires raising our children and wards in the right environment and not doing their jobs for them. By so doing, they will not only be making their own identities in life but will also earn and know the value of self-respect. Let us allow the oncoming generation to grow up and move forward. Allow them to visualise where they are going; then they will pack only what they need. Wrong advice and enforcement will lead them to wrong places and make them fall. As leaders and mentors, let us show the light and people will find their ways.

All thanks to God for the gift of the Holy Bible. As a scholar, I find the life stories of Prophet Elijah and his ward-cum-servant Prophet Elisha very interesting. To me, it is not who they were individually but collectively. They were both disciplinarians, and they were both guided by their passion for the work of God. They did not assume the responsibilities of parenthood in Israel. They were great prophets, bold, strong and courageous even on to death.

When Elisha set out as a servant to Elijah, he had nothing, as he gave all his possessions up. By following Elijah, he faced his place of challenge, a place of uncertainty, squarely. We will find our ways and fulfil our purpose in life only if we confront our scary places. Confrontation is the way to clear confusion.

Prophet Elijah was instructed by God to look for, find and appoint Elisha as his replacement: **1 Kings, Chapter 19 (verses 15 - 19): "And the Lord said unto Elijah, Go, return on thy way to the wilderness of Damascus; ...and Elisha the son of Shaphat of Abelmeholah shalt thou anoint to be prophet in thy room.**

So he departed thence, and found Elisha the son of Shaphat, who was ploughing with twelve yoke of oxen before him, and he with the twelfth: and Elijah passed by him and cast his mantle upon him". No deviation, no confusion, just direction. What God says will go against the natural. God had put Elisha's blessings in Elijah, and he released the blessings willingly and unconditionally. Elijah, by laying his mantle on Elisha, activated the Holy Spirit in him.

The process for Elisha was tedious and rough but he accomplished his goal. His investment of submission to his master and hard work yielded to greatness. Elisha stayed with his teacher, through thick and thin, to the end. We have to earn respect through what we go through.

In the **Book of 2nd Kings, Chapter 2, verses 9 – 10: "And it came to pass, when they had gone over, that Elijah said unto Elisha, Ask what I shall do for thee, before I be taken away from thee. And Elisha said, I pray thee, let a double** portion of thy spirit be upon me. And he said, Thou hast asked a hard thing: nevertheless, if thou see me when I am taken from thee, it shall be so unto thee; but if not, it shall not be so."

CHAPTER THREE

APPOINTING AND ANOINTING POWERS

Anointing power rests mainly with God. It is neither hereditary nor saleable.

If you are still here, in your place, not giving up, not running away, even when going through the highs and the lows, and remain cool in crisis, then and only then will you receive the power. The mantle will not fall until the moment is right.

Our life is the direct reflection of who we listen to. Elisha had received something from his teacher that changed his life.

The chariot's windows opened for Elijah's girdle

to fall on Elisha. God is ready to open for us His windows of blessings. It takes God to open doors and place people in His positions of authority. While we humans enthrone a king to rule over our domains, God ordains His clergymen. The heavens do rule in the affairs of man.

We are what we were formed into by God. The **Book of Jeremiah Chapter 1 (verses 4 - 5) reads: "Then the word of the Lord came unto me, saying; Before I formed thee in the belly I knew thee, and before thou camest forth out of the womb, I sanctified thee, and I ordained thee a prophet unto the nations."**

We must desist from creating positions for our children within the House of God. That is not within our power and reach.

In the Book of St. Matthew, Chapter 20 (verse 20): **"Then came to Jesus the mother of Zebedee's children with her sons, worshipping Him, and desiring a certain thing of Him. .... Grant that these my two sons may sit, one on thy right hand, and the other on the left, in thy kingdom".** That was a mother's request. We are all now behaving like this woman, busy pushing our children into positions not meant for them, just for our selfish ends, because we want a secured future thinking that if our children's future is secured, we are guaranteed our livelihood. We prepare them to be our meal tickets.

Money is the very thing that brings blessings, and it is also the very thing that brings the curse.

We are living on the purpose of our future security. This is a global social problem amongst church leaders. If this is our main aim, then Christianity has no great future in our land because Christ is not for sale and the roles in His Church are not securities for our old age pensions. We cannot have prosperity in nature until we get it in spirit. Just as Moses cut the solid rock tablets himself, we must work for it, sweat for it, labour over it, and invest in it in order to earn it.

The mother of Zebedee's children did not even discuss her wishes with her sons before making a request on their behalf. She assumed that because they were her sons, she knew what was good for them. She was an ignorant bully. The children had no say in matters concerning their lives. She was forcing her children into places not destined for them, but thank God, Christ pulped them out. Don't let your behaviour frustrate the grace of God in your life.

Like most mothers, if not all, we like to hear our own voices when asserting instructions. As a mother, with a bit of sobbing and a few drops of tears, I sprinkle a little of my magic dust around my children when giving them advisory sessions. Though I leave room for arguments, I am more stubborn than any of them because I have had more time to practise it. A little bit of persuasion wins them over even on matters relating to their careers and partners. Mothers tend to know best, but most of the time we are successfully wrong.

However, in Zebedee's case, the Lord puts her in her place. Christ had already touched and called her children.

His response to her request could be found in the following verses of Matthew, Chapter 20; 22 – 23: "But Jesus answered and said "Ye know not what ye ask. Are ye able to drink of the cup that I shall drink of, and to be baptized with the baptism that I am baptized with?" "....It is not mine to give; but it shall be given to them for whom it is prepared of my Father". We must stop putting our children under pressure and give them room to grow. We were predestined and pre-ordained before we were born. There is a process for our destiny. We must all go through it; no jumping ahead. It is best to wait on the Lord and do it in God's way. Encourage them to do what they are good at so that their works will show how good they are.

The actions of the mother of Zebedee's children were cruel, unnecessary and spiteful to the other Apostles. They were all waiting on Christ and serving Him, but by virtue of her closeness to Christ and her position in the community, she took it upon herself to elevate her children above the others. She overestimated her position, and Christ's response to her shows every one of us how fragile our ego is.

In life, whenever you are going to another level, you will need a sponsor; someone who points you out work and has been watching and witnessing it will introduce you to the next stage in life. Figure out where you are and who your sponsor is, because he or she may not necessarily be your parent.

CHAPTER FOUR

PARENTAL COMMITMENT

In the **Book 1st Samuel, Chapter 1 (verse 11):
"And she vowed a vow, and said, O Lord of
Host, if thou wilt indeed look at the affliction
of thine handmaid, and remember me and not
forget thine handmaid, but wilt give unto thine
handmaid a man child, then I will give him unto
the Lord all the days of his life, and there shall
no razor come upon his head"**.

Hannah, desperate to have a child, made a
vow before God that if her request for a son could
be granted, she would dedicate him to serve God
throughout his life. This was a lifelong commitment
even before birth. When you throw yourself into a

task unselfishly, God replenishes and repays you for your efforts.

She had been attending the feast and presenting her request to God for many years without any result. Sometimes a battle has to be fought many times before you win it. Hannah's prayer was a prayerful dialogue between Heaven and Earth; God and man. Her prayers strengthened the existing relationship and intimacy between her and God.

Eli, who had earlier mistakenly thought she was drunk, released words of blessings into her life and she claimed them. When we speak totality into our existence, our wish becomes real. As a clergyman, one must be aware and mindful of what the congregation is going through; their concerns. We must not be ignorant of their pains.

Rejoicing in the hope of the glory of God, Hannah immediately got up and had something to eat, and her attitude changed positively. A good lesson for us all is that to survive every calamity, we must rejoice in the hope of God. We will always be tested in an area we cannot fix ourselves. The real test of faith is to rejoice in tribulation. Eventually Hannah became pregnant and later gave birth to a male child, Samuel. God's process looked slow but sure.

Before ever Samuel was conceived, his life had been planned and sealed by Hannah, his mother, who did not allow flesh to talk her out of faith and vow. She brought the child Samuel to Eli, the Servant of God, and dedicated him there and then as she promised. God later blessed Hannah with five other children. Sometimes God will fix our situation just for His service.

By Samuel's dedication and services in the presence of God, we see the unification of parenthood and priesthood.

In the **Book of 1st Samuel, Chapter 1 (verse 26) – "And the child Samuel grew on, and was in favour both with the Lord, and also with him."**

Also, **1st Samuel, Chapter 2 (verses 1 - 10) summarising the Calling of Samuel – "And the child Samuel ministered unto the Lord... Then Samuel answered, Speak, for thy servant heareth".**

Clearly, the young will not achieve without leadership because leaders teach the oncoming generation not only how to respond but also show what to do to help themselves to achieve their destiny. Truly, the new broom may sweep better, but it is the old one that knows the nooks and corners of the house. We learn to live on the shelter of each other. When we share our memories with those coming behind, we help in creating new ones.

CHAPTER FIVE

FRAUDULENT HOPES

As an elderly Church Minister, I have seen instances of parents intentionally given their children fraudulent hopes. We must drum into their heads the realisation that their career is in fighting God's battles, but they are not alone as they fight alongside heavenly hosts. They are not in the service for wealth accumulation. This is the greatest advisory contribution towards their career.

We can share out of the abundance of what we have. As parents and mentors, what we instil in and share with our peers will be passed down to the general populace. As our thoughts determine our feelings, we must ensure and endure to care for all people, especially those in the congregation. Quite often, we the clergymen are the immediate answer to our parishioners' plights. Always, we must remember that we are dealing with people, not projects and paperwork. A bit of sacrifice made towards people's welfare will increase the value accorded to our contributions. Even if after all our contributions we still face rejection by the very people we are pasturing, we should not allow their action to undermine our value.

In the congregation, we are bound to face rejection. The very people you help will walk away from you without any acknowledgement. If after you touched them with care and kindness they do not change but still see themselves as miserable opponents, then my advice is to let them go. It has been predestined that you would render the assistance to them. Do your part truly and whole heartedly. The steps of a righteous man have been ordered by the Lord. You may feel used and abused, but do not get bitter. Rejection is part of the pain you bear when you carry your cross in stewardship. Count it as an experience of life in your eagerness to be in a relationship with your God. Forget those bad things that are behind you but reach out for better things in front of you, your future and destiny. A word of advice for oncoming clergy: whatever condition you find yourselves in, live for tomorrow and face the future. Forgive and release those who offend you. Give yourself a gift – forgiveness. Stop protecting yourself from people who do not matter. We humans are not all the same, we are created differently.

So, look after and take care of the remaining people in the fold. They are the ones whose destiny is tied to you. They believe in you, and that is why they support you.

Devote your time to making the congregation happy. Do not push them away. You cannot grow if you are afraid to be vulnerable.

Take care, be self-conscious, but do not be overprotective and selfish. Do not allow selfishness to kill your dreams and your success.

Even elderly, experienced and deep-rooted ministers still have strong ideas about deserters and at times question why. My answer is that it is natural. I find it provocative as well when the very people you devote your life to help decide to stab you in the back. So it has been from the beginning. In the **Book of 1st Samuel, Chapter 12, verse 3: "Behold, here I am: witness against me before the Lord, and before his anointed: whose ox have I taken? Or whose ass have I taken? Or whom have I defrauded? Whom have I oppressed? Or of whose hand have I received any bride to blind my eyes therewith?"**

His was a spine-tingling case because he started serving the people of God right from the tender age of childhood, only to be rejected at adulthood.

However, as stewards in the service of God, it costs what it costs to serve the Lord and to do the things He has called us to do. Serving and worshipping God is our priority. We have been given the title of stewards, and so we must do the job, investing everything in our possession in order to succeed. Our time, money, energy and life must be totally submitted to stewardship and service. We cannot give God a part and expect all. To receive all, we must first give all.

Bearing the weight of our cross is a must for us, because it is only by so doing that we shall rise up to overcome oppression, victimisation and rejection.

CHAPTER SIX

PASTORAL SORCERERS AND SOOTHSAYERS

Like everything else in life, experience is knowledge and wealth. If I share my own experience, the oncoming pastors, priests and spiritualists will benefit immensely.

Present day money-mongering pastors are in big trouble because greediness for wealth has taken over their lives. Basing their family financial stability on the Church, some just figure out who they want to be and live it. Not all are God-sent or chosen.

The Holy Bible gives examples of money-making devices that man indulges in. In the **Acts of the**

Apostles, Chapter 8 (9 -25) reads: **"But there was a certain man called Simon, which beforetime in the same city used sorcery, and bewitched the people of Samaria, giving out that himself was some great one"**. He approached and offered the Apostles money to purchase the Holy Spirit. Verse 20 reads: **"But Peter said unto him, thy money perish with thee, because thou has thought that the gift of God may be purchased with money"**.

These sorcery acts now engulf the so-called modern-day Christianity. Self-proclaiming Ministers are willing to go to any extent to acquire power, all in the name of fame and prosperity. These are the magicians of our time. Please do not be either amazed or impressed by them. By trickery, they drag people into their nets, by manipulating their victims' minds, making them see and do what they want. These sorcerers are instruments of the devil. Do not underestimate their strength. They take and steal from the ignorant and innocent who unfortunately find themselves in the wrong spiritual environment. They conjure, predict and foretell, but their ceremonial rites can never take the place of a Christian ministry.

The Book of **Acts of the Apostles, Chapter 16 (16 – 17), reads: "And it came to pass, as we went to prayer, a certain damsel possessed with a spirit of divination met us, which brought her masters much gain by soothsaying"**. This girl was practising sorcery for her masters, thereby making and bringing in money daily for their use. Their financial stability was practically based on sorcery.

Modern Day Magicians

Nowadays, there are some fake church ministers who are using their sorcery powers to perform miracles and deliverances and deceive innocent believers, all in the name of Jesus Christ. They use strange invocations, verses and knowledge to conjure spirits known only to them. Their drive for materialism, money, personal recognition and authority is disturbing. Nothing is spiritual about their sweetly-coated preaching and practice. They give "polished performances" when they are at the pulpit.

As clergymen and workers in the Lord's vineyard, we need to be surrounded by people who are truly seeking God, not just takers. Also, we need elder statemen, pastors and even parents who have talents that can actually help. They should be with their children and students bearing stress, pressure and responsibilities with them.

However, the present-day mentors are puppet masters hiding behind the screen and pulling the strings. Their agenda is mainly economic, not spiritual. Their Christianity is different from biblical teachings; theirs is influenced by creed and power domination. They are financially and politically charged ministers, corrupt to the core. They see the Church as a place of money making. Any opportunity to extract money from the congregation is to them a blessing, and they are ready and prepared at any time to loot, going to any extent in acquiring devilish powers. Unfortunately their wards are trapped to where they are and bound by those who raised them. Once in their deadly lion's den and trap, it is almost impossible for them to be released, and if eventually they are ever going to be released, it will take great courage. Those who dare may face trials, tribulations and destitution which may result in death.

I have a piece of advice for anyone who unfortunately finds himself in such a nasty and deadly situation. Do not be bitter, do not be desperate for vengeance, but just accept that their part in your life is over. Do not go back to them. As a man or woman of God, do not let people put you in a religious position so that they can have their way with you. Rather the closer you are to God, the further away you will be from your past puppet masters.

We owe our wards truth and guidance. In developing a relationship with them, we must not abuse their trust. Do not put your vision into your ward's head. Do not tie your destiny to your ward.

In a process of transformation, give the young ones the chance to think and choose for themselves. It is only by so doing they will become who they want to be.

Our children and wards are pregnant with possibilities. They will be transformed by the renewal of their minds. Free thinking makes us what we are. Let them absorb from the world around them what will lead them to their core, because we are effective by the world around us. The decisions we make determine who we are.

Finding the will of God for your child or ward is good, but preparing and compelling them to be who you want for your selfish gain is an abomination, just as living happily and extravagantly on ill-gotten wealth is. The future of the selfish dies for them.

CHAPTER SEVEN

THE YOUNG PASTOR AND THE EVIL MASTER

Some months ago, the story had it that a certain young pastor who was groomed, trained and eventually positioned in a city-based church came to his untimely death mysteriously.

He had started well and was settled with a young family of his own. The church progressed for a while. After a few years, the congregation was in decline; offerings were reduced and the pastor could not send his monthly remittance to headquarters. The situation grew from bad to worse despite all his efforts. He blamed God for being the source of his circumstances, and his family and himself for things not working right. He began to doubt his calling; he submitted to the spirit of fear and limited himself. Sometimes God pulls us back a bit to shoot us a long way forward. It is called catapulting. God blesses all.

This young pastor had a vision, but was without the strength to accomplish it. Take my advice, brethren, do not judge yourself prematurely.

In a situation such as this, the best solution is to continue praying till our faith is stirred up. Everybody has struggles and issues to deal with. There is no chance to fail if we do not give up. If you give up on yourself, you have no one and nowhere else to go. Reject frustration and discouragement, but continue praising and trusting God.

To succeed, we need perseverance, planning, hard work and be around people who lift us up. We need to let our followers and parishioners know who we are and when we are in a storm that we do not deserve or expect, they will rally round us.

The young pastor was astonished because he could see that his colleagues were better off than himself despite the fact that they were not fully dedicated. Riding flashy cars and hosting lavish parties, they were the flamboyant pastors. He felt alone and abandoned whilst his fellow ministers were comfortable enjoying their illicit wealth. Sometimes in life, if you want to be strong, you fight alone.

Desperate for a solution, he allowed his own personal ambition to take over. He confided in one of his colleagues, who advised him that in order to live comfortably like his fellow ministers, he had to join their inner circle, be in unity with his mates and try a new way of life. His friend jokingly advised him not to be a "one-man band" but to be part of the orchestra. He promised to speak to their Chief Pastor, the King of the Hills, who would approve his membership and release some "extra divination powers" to help him. Be careful not to look for comfort in a disturbing circle. Aspiring to live like your neighbour is dangerous. Do not compare yourself with anyone; you do not have the same starting place.

From my own personal experience, I know for sure that if God has ordered your steps, so also has He ordered your troubles. The troubles we are in are being used as pruning. The pruning process is tough and rough, but the end results are truly dazzling and joyful. To be a believer and an overcomer, one must acknowledge that delay is not a denial and whatever is blocking our destiny will be uprooted.

On his friend's intervention, this young man left his post and travelled down south to seek help from the Chief Pastor. His heart was right within him but amongst wrongful and woeful people. He was sincere, but sincerely wrong. A good boy in a bad company. Until the power inside of you is stronger than what is outside pursuing you, there will be no breakthrough.

The Chief Pastor was a rattlesnake; there was nothing good in him. He was treating the pastors under him like runny-nosed kids. He spoke eloquently to entice victims into his satanic web. Welcoming this young innocent pastor, with a gripping handshake, all his fears were brushed away by this evil senior pastor with promises of instant progress and elevation. Beware of promises written with water.

All he had to do was to have a midnight initiation ceremony at the seaside. He gave him a fraudulent hope and encouraged him to lose his innocence. This Chief Pastor passed his mistakes to his ward, luring the innocent into an amalgamation of sorcery and witchcraft. Who will pay when crimes become legal? For every decision we make, there are consequences.

The following day, at the appointed time, the young pastor and his master were at the seaside for the ceremony. Apparently, the master was a regular caller and he knew what to do. He conjured some spiritual beings from the sea and had dialogues with them in "a coded communication". The junior pastor was presented as a new convert, paid his membership fees by offering ten cowries and had sexual intercourse with the mermaid. Troubles bring strange bedfellows.

Because the junior pastor regarded this elderly minister as a father figure and trusted him wholeheartedly, he complied with all instructions given – blind trust. Do not worship at the shrine of traditionalism.

Before leaving the seaside, the mermaid gave her new conquest some items, including a pair of magical white handkerchiefs. These he would be waving on his congregation during revivals, and the spirit of ecstasy would fall on them.

On returning home he never mentioned anything to his wife about this turn of fate. Although they were in the house together, there was a deafening silence around them. It is a man's world! Some people have a tendency to react arrogantly to problems. Humility is the first sign of submission.

As instructed, on getting back to his post, he tested all the charms he had been given and found them performing wonders and miracles. He became full of himself, boastful and arrogant. These deceitful miracles were televised locally. With pride, he referred to himself as an extraordinary pastor because of the miracles he claimed to be performing. Publicly, he told his congregation that ordinariness is the enemy of miracles. From a true believer, he turned to become a true deceiver. You become what you talk about.

He began speaking two sinfully indulging languages – money and fame. His love turned to lust. When at the pulpit, he wanted to be admired and praised. He even had a slogan for himself: **"Favour is better than labour"**. There is no room in the mind that is full of itself. Pride became his adorning, choking collar, as he was now seen as the talk of the town and the envy of his friends. People began to sing his praises, and he enjoyed every moment of it. Be very careful about praise singers. Do not be defiled by hailing praises or excited about their recognition. If you ascend by their praises, your descent will surely be sung by them.

The church congregation grew in number and money started rolling in again. But after six months, the congregation scattered and left; the old problem resurfaced. This time around, the master behind the curtain asked him back to base and the solution this time was to sleep with young innocent virgins. He was led deeper and deeper into occult secrecy by his master, but he was too scared to challenge his senior pastor. You cannot free people if you are bound with the same chains.

Whilst all this were going on, the young pastor completely forgot his Holy Bible and the power of God in him. The use of charms made his life easier; he totally depended on it. He called himself a miracle worker, but he was only performing magic tricks and illusions. You are attracted to what you are exposed to. Whatever you yield yourself to the most, is what you become. But nothing lasts forever, except the Grace of God. His fragile state of peace and affluence was over. Just as he reached the height of his manmade success, he experienced a disastrous downfall. His marriage was the first thing to break; he lost two sons and his post. His situation became too difficult for him to cope with. He looked severely tortured and haggard. He failed woefully, and his failure brought him to his knees. He was where he was because of the choices he had made.

On seeing that he had run out of options and that the end had come, at the last stage of desperation he remembered to pray and to read the Holy Bible, the Word of God which is the life-giving power of God. But God does not talk through contaminated sources. Our God is not the author of confusions. You cannot fix it at the corner after breaking it in public.

Unfortunately the junior pastor died mysteriously just some days after coming out with his story. His dreams died on the way without accomplishment. Some people said that he fainted in his mind and died without encouraging himself. Other said he committed suicide. Many said he was silenced. Whichever way, he died. It hurts when you end up with misery whilst expecting a miracle; that is the death of expectation.

An advisory note to oncoming ministers is to have very clear self-perception so as to minimise their dependency of other people. Understand who you are and see yourself correctly in order to overcome any battle ahead of you. Know and understand the purpose of your calling. What happens in life matters, but what matters most is our understanding of every circumstance. I pray for God to give us the eyes and mind of understanding.

The wrong people will lead you to the wrong places and may result to stumbling. Do not waste time competing with other people. Sometimes the people around you may not be under your vision.

Set a goal for yourself and achieve it. Avoid circumstances that are against achieving your goal. What God gave you is unique to you only.

Try and take your talents to the next level. Our teaching and preaching should influence our living styles. God will only bless what we are, not what we pretend to be.

Do not be deceived by manipulations. Self-pity and deceit are like constantly declaring that you are watching your weight while eating your meals in front of the mirror!

Accept that you are different from others. God created you to be different.

In life, we may find ourselves in situations where we flap and fall. Yet God always uses such circumstances for our progression.

Talking to you, the reader, do you find yourself in a similar situation to that described above? Are you groaning under a heavy weight? Do you feel lonely, abandoned and scared? Then let the Holy Spirit intercede. He knows your mind as well as the mind of God. He prays to God on our behalf. The Holy

Spirit figures everything out thoroughly, emotionally, physically and spiritually.

Our connection with the Holy Spirit increases our faith and understanding. Let us form an amicable association with the Holy Spirit and humbly pray to God for help. Let us study the Holy Bible and keep the words of life in our heads. It is only by so doing that we can by faith speak to our condition and change the way we see and talk to ourselves; bless and prophesy positively into our lives. It is what we say that will determine what is going to happen to us.

The storm of life comes out from nowhere; nobody is too small or big to have a problem. If it comes after you, God has given it permission. Everything comes from God, blessings, struggles and intimidation. We all have thorns to bear in our flesh which we are not prepared to accept. However, sometimes the punch we receive serves as a servant to our destiny. God can use our pain as a test to balance our success with humility, so what we regard as a pain may serve as a gift in disguise.

When problems arise, never rely on your strength or resources; rather depend on God for victory. Do not be full of pride and rebellion. Our dependency on God cements our relationship and association with Him.

CHAPTER 8

STEWARDSHIP REWARDS

Good solicitors must be conversant with the constitution of the country in order to represent their clients. Similarly, good clerics and church ministers, apart from spiritual inspiration, must be fluent and well-versed in biblical and religious doctrines. You can only share out of what you possess. The urge for knowledge drives me to read and study more.

Whilst studying the Holy Bible, the lives of some of the men and women of God and their personal encounters made me choke with grief.

At the beginning, Aaron's calling was good. He was an obedient servant of God, a willing partner to his brother Moses, his mouthpiece and keeper. The Holy

Bible confirms that Aaron was always in the presence of God as a Priest of the Most High, constantly serving in His Temple. The **Book of 1st Chronicles, Chapter 6, verse 49 reads: "But Aaron and his sons offered upon the altar of the burnt offering, and on the altar of incense, and were appointed for all the work of the place most holy, and to make atonement for Israel, according to all that Moses the servant of God had commanded."**

However, two incidents in his life brought me to tears. Firstly, two of his sons dropped dead, right there in the presence of God, in the Temple. The **Book of Leviticus, Chapter 10, verses 1 – 3 reads: "And Nadab, and Abihu, the sons of Aaron, took either of them his censer, and put fire therein, and put incense thereon, and offered strange fire before the Lord, which he commanded them not. And there went out fire from the Lord, and devoured them, and they died before the Lord... and Aaron held his peace."** Aaron lost heavily during his stewardship. On our way to glory, losing stuff hurts deeply, thereby making our relationship with God fluctuate based on our circumstances.

The incident described above portrays in my mind a picture whereby the law shines the light on where the Lord draws the line. Nadab and Abihu, the sons of Aaron, brought 'strange fire' into the presence of

God, contravening the laid down instruction; for this, God struck them dead.

If the Lord is to apportion blame, who could stand against Him? Nobody. We are all guilty and rotten.

If this happened to any of us nowadays, how would we take it? We modern-day Christian believers do worse things. We bring strange doctrines, habits and strange people into the House of God. But the Grace of God, through Jesus Christ, upholds us. We lack the power to save ourselves. We need the Grace of God for the challenges we face. His lessons put us on the right path.

The second incident is also based on the life of Aaron, his death and the story behind it. As we know, Aaron, Miriam and Moses were blood brothers and sister, born of Jochebed, a daughter of Levi. They all served God in their various fields to their maximum capacity, and according to what they were destined to do. These great Prophets and Prophetesses of old were very good at what they did, and the children of Israel pointed them out to be excellent leaders. They were vibrantly in the presence of God and constant in worship, praises and thanksgiving.

The **Book of Exodus, Chapter 15, verses 20 and 21 reads: "And Miriam the prophetess, sister of Aaron, took a timbrel in her hand; and all the women went out after her with timbrels and with dances. And Miriam "answered them,**

'Sing ye to the Lord, for HE hath triumphed gloriously; the horse and its rider hath the Lord thrown into the sea".

This terrific, empowering woman sang praises to God, along with the grateful nation Israel, singing and dancing to the Living God.

What then went wrong with the stewardships of these three great servants of God?

In the case of Miriam, the elegant and gracious prophetess, she fell by the wayside because of her arrogance and pride. God left her because of her utterances. Miriam tried to express her personality. She developed a superwoman complex, forgetting that the holiness of God can never be commandeered, grabbed or defiled by anyone. You must break yourself to become humble, otherwise God will break you. If God stretches out to you, please melt into his hands with humility. Humility is the only way to exaltation.

In the case of the twosome Aaron and Moses, they were driven by the spirit of frustration. Being surrounded by the great pressure and responsibilities of leadership, beyond human comprehension and understanding, they were at breaking point.

We could say that by now, judging by the hardships faced in the desert, in their uncomfortable zone, by these two patriarchs, they would have got addicted to being uncomfortable.

According to the **Book of Numbers, Chapter 20, verses 8 -12: "And the Lord spoke unto Moses, saying; Take the rod, and gather thou the assembly together, thou and Aaron thy brother, and speak you unto the rock before their eyes; and it shall give forth his water and thou shall bring forth to them water out of the rock: so thou shall give the congregation and their beasts drink".**

And Moses took the rod from before the Lord, as He commanded him. And Moses and Aaron gathered the congregation together before the rock and he said unto them, Hear now ye rebels, must we fetch you water out of this rock?

"And Moses lifted up his hand, and with his rod he smote the rock twice and the water came out... And the Lord spoke unto Moses and Aaron, because you believed me not, to sanctify me in the eyes of the children of Israel, therefore ye shall not bring this congregation into the land which I have given them."

By striking the rock on his own initiative instead of speaking to it as directed by God, Moses disobeyed the Lord. The **Book of Deuteronomy, Chapter 28, verse 1 reads: "And it shall come to pass, if thou shall hearken diligently unto the voice of the Lord they God, to observe and to do all his commandments..."** You don't knock down the wall just because there is a crack in the plaster.

Both Moses and Aaron had warfare and a battleground in their minds, because they felt that the children of Israel were ungrateful for the help they had received. As humans, they had a grudge in mind against the people and a bone to pick with them. It is with the mind that we serve the Lord.

As humans, both Moses and Aaron might have felt criticised and victimised for working too hard. The two patriarchs might feel their punishment was excessive. However, we must learn to show appreciation for the opportunities we have and positions that we hold; we must not mess it up. Our discipleship work must be done truly and thoroughly with integrated deep affection and obedience. We must learn to work on our self-discipline at all levels. When you talk and preach to the congregation of God about emotions, you must control your own.

CHAPTER 9

UNEXPECTED VISITATIONS & REWARDS

The story of Obededom is a coded communication from God to all His servants and believers that He would visit us, expecting us to be ready to welcome Him into our households. The Lord comes quickly to reward us, and our oncoming generations, as we deserve. This is the highlight of Obededom's story.

Nothing was mentioned of Obededom's prior and constant stewardship in the presence of the Lord. Obededom was living on purpose. He was born to be effective in doing God's work.

The **Book of 1st Chronicles, Chapter 26 (verses**

8, and 15: "All these of the sons of Obededom; they and their sons and their brethren, able men for strength for the service, were threescore and two of Abededom. To Obededom southward; and to his sons the house of Assuppim" Obededom was a gatekeeper in the House of the Lord and so also were his sons. Obededom's sons followed their father because they saw favour in his life and that was why they were blessed. Our pastoral duties must engulf us and our household in order for us to have spiritual fulfilment in life.

Just like Obededom, our children, spouse and whole family must be supportive. They put everything they had into the service of God and likewise God put every goodness and mercies into their household. Favour was God's investment in Obededom's household. His household was not the only one around, but there was something about him that God could trust, and that was why He picked him.

Obededom had been in service practice as a Gatekeeper in the House of God. Everything he practised on was in preparation for God's glory in his life. By occupying his post as a Gatekeeper, God was setting him up into a mighty position that was greater than him. He was being shaped to fit into God's blessings. So when the Ark of God was brought to his house, Obededom knew what to do. He had been destined to walk and stand at attention before the Lord. God helped him to turn his duty into a useful service. Not everybody was highly blessed and favoured. Obededom invested human responsibility and participation in the work of God and God recognised and blessed his contributions.

The Ark of God was taken to and stayed harmlessly and peacefully in the house of a devoted Servant of God, Obededom, the Gatekeeper. And the Lord blessed him for his service. He was favoured to stand out, and elevated because he served the Lord. He was treated with grace, like a king. Obededom was worthy of every blessing God gave him.

Great lessons are for us in this story. God will bless us whilst training us. Do not sit on the gift God has given you. Whatever position you are appointed to in the Vineyard of God, perform your duties diligently. Be neither nasty nor lazy. Nastiness will lock you out of favour, and you cannot use prayers to replace laziness. To whom much is given, much is expected.

We modern-day Christians often think that prayers and fasting will replace our shortcomings. No, they will not replace our bad manners, decisions and attitudes. Just like Obededom, we must contribute something in order to enjoy merit. Whatever hardship we are facing now is preparing us for the purpose of favour in our life, and prosperity for future generations.

CHAPTER 10

THE POWER OF INTERCESSION

From time to time, advisory sessions are essential and helpful for our children and wards. They need to think highly of the people they are called to serve, because it is only by so doing that they will have the opportunity to grow.

Our wards must be refined to be the best in service to God and man, humbling themselves in order to be fit to serve. These advisory sessions must not be seen as judgemental or sentimental. Rather, they should be regarded and taken with a bit of friendly teasing. May God find us merciful rather than judgemental. Amen.

There is a need to understand the responsibilities

of our ministerial positions towards the congregation, but especially towards our young parish wardens and pastors. God has placed them in our care to feed them with the words of God and encourage them to be strong and resistant when facing spiritual ordeals.

The **Book of 1st Timothy, Chapter 5, verse 23: 'Drink no longer water, but use a little wine for thy stomach's sake and thine often infirmities'.** Here, St. Paul was recommending to Timothy, his ward, a little wine-drinking for medicinal purposes. Apostle Paul was only looking after the welfare of his ward, and this is worthy of emulation. Paul the Apostle was not being manipulative but rather nice, plain and truthful. So also must we likewise show ourselves friendly and caring to our children and our wards. They do have the ability to retain the kindness and transferable skills which we shower on them. Kindness is the language that the deaf can hear and the blind can see. Kindness is the only language which all the human and animal races understand.

With our parental and ministerial positions, we are grooming our children and wards and shaping them to step into powers and opportunities. Also, we are transferring our generational wealth of experience on to them. This will make their lives pleasant and the future inquisitively explorable. Sometimes the future is written in the past. There is a future beyond our life time.

Whatsoever we put in our wards and children will germinate. So also, prayers said on their behalf will be answered. There is power in our blessings and prayers to our children and wards.

Could King Solomon, out of his own discretion, asked God for the gift of wisdom and understanding probably because he had heard his father King David in intercessory prayers making such requests to God on his behalf? The Book of **1st Kings Chapter 3 (verses 7 – 9) reads: "And now, O Lord my God, thou hast made thy servant King instead of David my father; and I am but a little child. I know not how to go out or come in. And thy servant is in the midst of thy people... Give therefore thy servant an understanding heart to judge thy people, that I may discern between good and bad"**.

Here King Solomon's prayer teaches us one very valuable lesson. Reflect on things that matter most before you present your prayers to the Lord.

Could it be that his father King David, in his intercessional prayers for his son Solomon, prayed to God to please endow Solomon with wisdom? In the **Book of 1st Chronicles Chapter 29 (verse 19), King David rendered his prayer to God thus: "And give unto Solomon my son, a perfect heart, to keep your commandments, thy testimonies, and thy statutes, and to do all these things,**

and to build the palace, for which I have made provision".

It may be that King Solomon had seen his father praying and heard his intercessory prayers beforehand. When you see excellence in a new form, then you enlarge and perfect your own. In life, experience is knowledge and wealth.

So when God asked him to make his own request, Solomon followed his father's footstep. He asked for the greatest gift, one which surpasses the might of man - wisdom. This gift carried him to where no training could. King Solomon flew into his destiny. Never ask for little presents when in the presence of a King, and do not be satisfied too soon. God has in His hands blessings beyond measure.

We must take it as one of our duties to give advisory sessions to the oncoming ministers. We must keep on teaching and preaching; create teaching avenues such as lecturers, Bible studies, song concerts, choir practice and other fact-finding expeditions, as these will open their spiritual eyes to the facts of life.

In the Holy Bible, **2nd Kings 6 (verses 17 – 20), Elisha prayed: "Open his eyes, Lord, so that he may see".** Then the Lord opened the servant's eyes and he looked and saw the hills full of horses. The servant saw the army of angels; he saw the presence of God, His protection and provision. Who intercedes for you?

Whatever we need to survive any situation around us is in us, not around us.

As Church Ministers and leaders, we must examine ourselves to understand what is in us. Whatever in us is what we pass on to those we are raising to replace us.

The Centurion, in the **Book of St Luke, Chapter 7 (verses 1-10), came to Jesus pleading with him for healing, on behalf of his servant. "And when he heard of Jesus, he sent him the elders of the Jews, beseeching him that he would come and heal his servant".**

This Centurion set a good example for all human beings to let us emulate him. There is nothing like being at the right place at the right time. We must care for those around us, especially those whom we lead.

The story of the Daughter of Jairus **(Luke 8 : 40-56): "Now when Jesus returned, a crowd welcomed him, for they were expecting him. Then a man named Jairus, a synagogue leader, came and fell at Jesus's feet, pleading with him to come to his house because his only daughter, a girl of twelve, was dying".**

We have people who speak for us behind closed doors. Fellows in the vineyard of Christ, we are blessed to serve as spiritual sponsors to our wards and children. We speak for them behind closed doors, in meditation, pleading, and constant prayers. Just like Jairus, we must rush out, crawling, crying and seeking for Christ for the salvation of our Wards and children.

We have been positioned correctly by God, just like King David, Elisha, the Centurion and Jairus, as a fortress for the safety of the coming generation. God has used our life experience for divine purposes. In grooming the oncoming servants of our Lord and God, we let them share from our own wealth of experience. They need not suffer as we did. They can get what we have got without going through the rigours, hatred and storms of life. We pray for God to open their vision and our joint efforts will help them to accomplish their mission. That is the part we are to play in their life.

Holy Spirit Intercessions

We are serving a God of revelations, and it is through the Holy Spirit that God sends messages to us. The Holy Spirit knows all supernatural facts. He searches the deep things of God and reveals them to us. The Holy Spirit is the all-knowing person. He gives us wisdom and insight, therefore what God has for us will be revealed by the Holy Spirit. He can communicate with us in various ways, in our bellies, our dreams and our heads, by healing and so on. All we need to do is just to believe that if we receive it in spirit it will happen in reality. When God speaks it in our spirit, then we receive with faith before it materialises in the natural world.

Conclusively, services in the Christ's vineyard have given me a majestic look and great pleasures. Crazy and wretched as I am, and without any outstanding quality at all, God still uses me. What a privilege!

As a parent and also a Minister in the Lord's vineyard, I think we have been put in charge of our children and wards so that we can learn precious lessons from training them. When we fill them up with our knowledge and experience, then God refills us. Our training in life continues as we put Him first in life; He will continue to empower and bless us. May we be closely knitted together by God with his Love.

May we all be referred and respected in our various dedicated services in Jesus Christ's vineyard. Amen.

www.ingramcontent.com/pod-product-compliance
Lightning Source LLC
Chambersburg PA
CBHW060716030426
42337CB00017B/2885